THIS BOOK BELONGS TO

, ,

By CAREEM BUFFET

"What is lovely never dies,
but passes into another
loveliness, Star-dust or sea-
foam, Flower or winged air."
– Thomas Bailey Aldrich

•"I don't think looking at things through the prism of fear is going to accomplish anything."
-- **Rush Limbaugh**

•"I want the largest audience I can get, because that's how I can charge the highest advertising rate. Which means what else do I want? Money. I am trying to earn a profit. It's capitalism."
-- **Rush Limbaugh**

•"I don't think looking at things through the prism of fear is going to accomplish anything."
-- **Rush Limbaugh**

- "In a country of children where the option is Santa Claus or work, what wins?"
-- **Rush Limbaugh**

•"I'd get up in the morning, get ready to go to school, and I would dread it. I hated it. My mother would have the radio on. And the guy on the radio sounded like he was having so much fun. And I knew, when his program was over, he wasn't going to go to school."
-- **Rush Limbaugh**

•"Football is like life and I know life."
-- **Rush Limbaugh**

•"My family is all lawyers. Most people when they come on shows like this, "I'm proud of the first member of my family to get a college education.""
-- **Rush Limbaugh**

_____

•"How many of you guys, in your own experience with women, have learned that no means yes if you know how to spot it?"
-- **Rush Limbaugh**

• "I have a practice of really not talking about the competition. I'm from the old school."
-- **Rush Limbaugh**

- "If Thomas Jefferson thought taxation without representation was bad, he should see how it is with representation."
-- **Rush Limbaugh**

•"And one of the things that makes me happiest and proudest is that the talk radio venue, the whole market has expanded. There are all kinds of people doing it."
-- **Rush Limbaugh**

•"What's the difference between a liberal and a conservative? A liberal will interpret the constitution, a conservative will quote it!"
-- **Rush Limbaugh**

•"Psychologically, when I sit down at noon, I'm it. I'm the only thing on. Nobody else does what I do. Nobody else has the opportunity. That's the psychological mindset. It's not an ego thing; it's just the way I've always approached it."
-- **Rush Limbaugh**

•"What is it with all of these young, single white women? Overeducated- doesn't mean intelligent."
-- **Rush Limbaugh**

•"I am sort of proud that I think radio has become a dominant influence in shaping public opinion. Good radio paints the picture for the audience. The audience has to be actively involved. Sometimes, in television, you can get lulled into sleep watching the picture, not listening to what you're hearing."
-- **Rush Limbaugh**

•"You know why there's a Second Amendment? In case the government fails to follow the first one."
-- **Rush Limbaugh**

•"The media uses polls to create news stories. I think polls are just an extension of the editorial page, an excuse to get them on the front page. You can ask any question you want, get any answer you want, and then run around with that as a news story."
-- **Rush Limbaugh**

•"When WOMEN got the right to vote is when it all went downhill. Because that's when votes started being cast with emotion and uh, maternal instincts that government ought to reflect..."
-- **Rush Limbaugh**

•"I come from a long ago era where men could be men and stereotypical humor didn't offend anybody."
-- **Rush Limbaugh**

•"Liberals believe that crime is inextricably linked with poverty. In reality, most poor people never resort to crime, and some wealthy people commit evil acts to enrich themselves further. Harlem, East Los Angeles, the South side of Chicago are not the poorest communities in the United States. According to a new U.S. Bureau of the Census report, the poorest communities are Shannon County, South Dakota, followed by Starr, Texas, and Tunica, Mississippi. Have you ever heard of these residents rioting to protest their living conditions?"
-- **Rush Limbaugh**

•"If people are speaking about something passionately and if they have a level of intelligence about it and if they're sufficiently informed, it's going to be like a magnet to people."
-- **Rush Limbaugh**

•"The First Amendment doesn't give anybody the right to be heard. People don't have to listen to you."
-- **Rush Limbaugh**

• "Barack Obama doesn't think this country should be number one. If it were number 35 it'd be fine with him."

-- **Rush Limbaugh**

•"By government giveaway programs, individuals are often hurt far more than they are helped. The recipients of these programs become dependent on the government and their dignity is destroyed. Is it compassionate to enslave more and more people by making them a part of the government dependency cycle? I think compassion should be measured by how many people no longer need it. Helping people to become self-sufficient is much more compassionate than drugging them with the narcotic of welfare."
-- **Rush Limbaugh**

•"My friend Michael Reagan has given us the blueprint for a new Reagan revolution- and he has given Ronald Reagan back to us again. Read it, learn it, live it, love it!"
-- **Rush Limbaugh**

•"I'm amazed at the Democrats and the media who do not know what's going on in my world. I know what's going on in theirs. I study 'em. I watch 'em every day."
-- **Rush Limbaugh**

•"Poverty is not the root cause of crime."
-- **Rush Limbaugh**

•"Most of my critics don't even listen to me; they are clueless. They just go to Web sites that report what I say out of context."
-- **Rush Limbaugh**

•"I have found it to be true that the older I've become the better my life has become."
-- **Rush Limbaugh**

•"My objective is to satisfy [my] audience so they come back the next day."
-- **Rush Limbaugh**

•"The Republican Party, I really believe, suffers from post-traumatic stress disorder from years and years of bullying and taunting. The Republican Party is Jonathan Martin. The Democrat Party and the media are Richie Incognito."
-- **Rush Limbaugh**

•"The danger with mentioning names is that you hurt the feelings of people that you leave out."
-- **Rush Limbaugh**

• "The difference between Los Angeles and yogurt is that yogurt comes with less fruit."
-- **Rush Limbaugh**

•"The ocean will take care of this on its own if it was left alone and left out there. It's natural. It's as natural as the ocean water is."
-- **Rush Limbaugh**

•"Compassion is no substitute for justice."
-- **Rush Limbaugh**

•"Money is the fuel that makes political victory possible. Sadly, folks, in many cases it's more important than ideas. And this is what turns off so many people to politics."
-- **Rush Limbaugh**

•"Given the National Organization for Women's membership and proclivities, it's no wonder that people now view the NOW gang as being obsessed with only two issues: abortion rights and lesbian rights."
-- **Rush Limbaugh**

•"I must be honest. I can only read so many paragraphs of a New York Times story before I puke."
-- **Rush Limbaugh**

•"Canada has an immigration policy you might want to emulate. They want more skilled and educated immigrants. In fact, that's all they take. But, see, since nobody's watching them, and they're not a superpower, nobody really cares. So they are allowed to act in their best interests."
-- **Rush Limbaugh**

•"Socks is the White House cat. But did you know there is also a White House dog?"
-- **Rush Limbaugh**

- "The world's biggest problem is the unequal distribution of capitalism. If there were capitalism everywhere, you wouldn't have food shortages."
-- **Rush Limbaugh**

•"Kurt Cobain was, ladies and gentleman, I just--
he was a worthless shred of human debris..."
-- **Rush Limbaugh**

- "This is a frightening statistic. More people vote in 'American Idol' than in any US election."
  -- **Rush Limbaugh**

•"She comes to me when she wants to be fed. And after I feed her -- guess what -- she's off to wherever she wants to be in the house, until the next time she gets hungry. She's smart enough to know she can't feed herself. She's actually a very smart cat. She gets loved. She gets adoration. She gets petted. She gets fed. And she doesn't have to do anything for it, which is why I say this cat's taught me more about women, than anything my whole life."
-- **Rush Limbaugh**

•"When a gay person turns his back on you, it is anything but an insult; it's an invitation."
-- **Rush Limbaugh**

- "Character matters; leadership descends from character."
-- **Rush Limbaugh**

•<u>"Charity is willingly given from the heart."</u>
-- **<u>Rush Limbaugh</u>**

•"We're not sexists, we're chauvinists - we're male chauvinist pigs, and we're happy to be because we think that's what men were destined to be. We think that's what women want."
-- **Rush Limbaugh**

•"Being stuck is a position few of us like. We want something new but cannot let go of the old - old ideas, beliefs, habits, even thoughts. We are out of contact with our own genius. Sometimes we know we are stuck; sometimes we don't. In both cases we have to DO something."
-- **Rush Limbaugh**

•"The truth does not require a majority to prevail, ladies and gentlemen. The truth is its own power. The truth will out. Never forget that."
-- **Rush Limbaugh**

•"I think this reason why girls don't do well on multiple choice tests goes all the way back to the Bible, all the way back to Genesis, Adam and Eve. God said, 'All right, Eve, multiple choice or multiple orgasms, what's it going to be?' We all know what was chosen."
-- **Rush Limbaugh**

•<u>"You Know How To Stop Abortion? Require That Each One Occur With A Gun."</u>
-- **<u>Rush Limbaugh</u>**

•"I'm a huge supporter of women. What I'm not is a supporter of liberalism. Feminism is what I oppose. Feminism has led women astray. I love the women's movement â€" especially when walking behind it."

-- **Rush Limbaugh**

•"The only way to reduce the number of nuclear weapons is to use them."
-- **Rush Limbaugh**

•"Have you ever noticed how all composite pictures of wanted criminals resemble Jesse Jackson?"
-- **Rush Limbaugh**

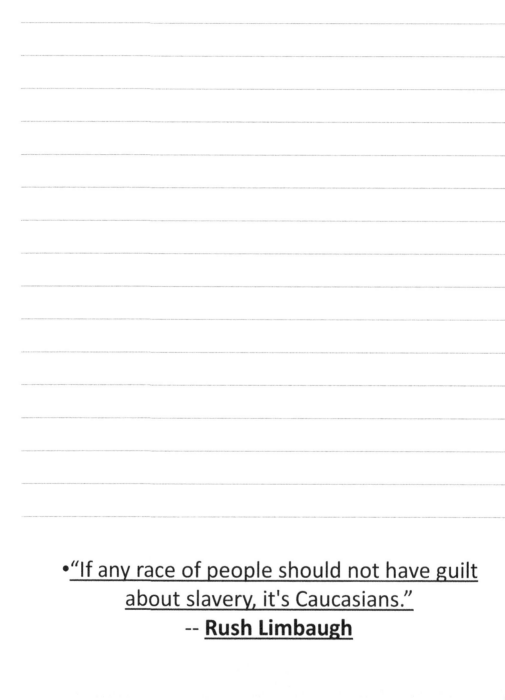

•"If any race of people should not have guilt about slavery, it's Caucasians."
-- **Rush Limbaugh**

•"Conservatism is not the problem. Conservatism is the founding of this country, essentially. Conservatism isn't even really an ideology. Conservatism is just what is right, proper, decent, and moral. That's all it is."
-- **Rush Limbaugh**

•"We live in a world of intolerance masked as tolerance."
-- **Rush Limbaugh**

•"This is so classic. Government comes along under the guise of fairness, fixes something, gonna make it fair, gonna make it equal, gonna make it affordable, maybe even make it free. What they end up doing is blowing it all to hell, screwing it up worse than it's ever been screwed up, then their voters bellyache and complain about it. And the same Democrats come back and demand that something be done, because their voters need a second chance."
-- **Rush Limbaugh**

•"I think cigars are just a tremendous addition to the enjoyment of life."
-- **Rush Limbaugh**

•"There isn't a single government agency that can't function. There's more money in this federal government, there's more money allocated than these people can possibly spend. They have to concoct asinine ways to spend it, like advertising for new food stamp users. I've gotten to the point, I'm just so righteously indignant and offended at the very idea that our government could ever run out of money when we've got a printing press, for crying out loud. Printed three and a half trillion dollars over seven years and flooded Wall Street with it."

-- **Rush Limbaugh**

•"If you ever find that you only have an hour to live .... spend it with a liberal and it will seem like a year."
-- **Rush Limbaugh**

•"Ladies, if you want a happy marriage, then do whatever your husband tells you without questioning his authority."
-- **Rush Limbaugh**

•<u>"For government to give, it must first take away."</u>
-- **<u>Rush Limbaugh</u>**

• "I am just stupefied here. The left has officially stamped it now: Oil is a villain. Now, please ask yourselves: When did this start?"
-- **Rush Limbaugh**

•"I don't know whether to admit it or not. You think I should tell them, Snerdley ? Okay. Folks, some good friends of mine who live here in Palm Beach bought a Smart Car... and there's a picture of me in it."
-- **Rush Limbaugh**

•"The vast majority of the rich in this country did not inherit their wealth; they earned it. They are the country's achievers, producers, and job creators."
-- **Rush Limbaugh**

•"Obama had the audacity to say, 'I have unequivocally prohibited the use of torture by the United States.' Ladies and gentlemen, torture in the United States has always been illegal."
-- **Rush Limbaugh**

•"Nobody in a leadership level in American politics is trying to inspire the American people. Everybody needs to be goosed. The vast majority of people are not self-starters."

• "Most people have this protective view of the presidency. Anybody who holds the office is always gonna get the benefit of the doubt unless the media spends four years destroying them like they did Bush, and with Bush not returning fire."

-- Rush Limbaugh

•"Most men would love to be stared at by women. Don't doubt me on this. And my guess is that most women are actually intrigued by it and have developed techniques and skills for dealing with it. Don't doubt me."
-- **Rush Limbaugh**

•"Most liberals I know do not consider themselves to even be liberals. They just think of you and me as conservatives, and that means, therefore, we're odd and we're kooks and maybe extreme and maybe mean."
-- **Rush Limbaugh**

•"So, Ms. Fluke and the rest of you feminazis, here's the deal: If we are going to pay for you to have sex, we want something for it, and I'll tell you what it is -- we want you to post the videos online so we can all watch."
-- **Rush Limbaugh**

•"So I shamelessly say, no, I want [Obama] to fail, if his agenda is a far-left collectivism, some people say socialism, as a conservative heartfelt, deeply, why would I want socialism to succeed?"

-- **Rush Limbaugh**

•"We have the most liberal, the most leftist candidate who has ever run for president in my lifetime; he's a sitting duck. This guy's policies are aimed at destroying the age of American greatness."
-- **Rush Limbaugh**

•"The fact that we're spending $700 billion a year on oil is actually a good thing; it means we have the prosperity to do it. It means that oil's being used, and oil is the fuel for the engine of freedom."
-- **Rush Limbaugh**

•"That cracker made a lot of African-American millionaires."
-- **Rush Limbaugh**

•"Everybody wants to be loved by everybody, and they'll do everything they can to be loved, including not be who they really are, from person to person."
-- **Rush Limbaugh**

•"Every Republican is on record as saying Obamacare is unacceptable, intolerable, and they're gonna do everything they could to keep it from happening. But, at the moment of truth, they're not."
-- **Rush Limbaugh**

•"Do you realize, when Mandela was inaugurated president, he invited as his special guests the white jailers from his Robben Island prison? He literally did forgive everybody."
-- **Rush Limbaugh**

•"Democrat women lead the way in showing other women how to be stepped on and diminished by men. That's what they do, for a payoff somewhere down the line."
-- **Rush Limbaugh**

•"By the way, I don't mean to pick nits here, but Obama has just ordered the flag at half-mast for 10 days for Mandela. He did not order the flag at half-mast at all for Lady Thatcher."
-- **Rush Limbaugh**

•"Being a conservative union member is almost like being an actor in Hollywood: You don't dare say it, or you might be injured on the job, or you might be laid off, or your family might have something happen to them."
-- **Rush Limbaugh**

•"As far as I'm concerned, the people who aren't paying taxes don't get to run around claiming that they built everything, that the built the roads and that they built the bridges and so forth."
-- **Rush Limbaugh**

•"A United States collapse would be much different than a Greece collapse. Greece can collapse, and there's a ripple. We collapse, and the world feels it."
-- **Rush Limbaugh**

•"A bunch of liberals wanted to outlaw men gazing at women because the gaze was said to objectify women. Sorry, liberals, it can't be helped among the heterosexual crowd."
-- **Rush Limbaugh**

•"As far as the media's concerned, Mrs. Obama deserves this. Look at the sordid past. Look at our slave past, look at the discriminatory past. It's only fair that people of color get their taste of the wealth of America too."
-- **Rush Limbaugh**

•"There's nothing to Obama - nothing but platitudes. When it's time to get to the substance, we get contradictions and confusions. We don't think that he knows what he's talking about because it's true: He doesn't."
-- **Rush Limbaugh**

•"I go back and forth as to whether I think Nancy Pelosi's really this dumb or not. Although, every time I hear her speak I get closer and closer to concluding that she is this dumb."
-- **Rush Limbaugh**

•"What we need to do is stop global warming; that's the only way to stop your peanut butter cups from melting. And if that doesn't do the trick, then put them in the fridge. Or better yet, eat them."
-- **Rush Limbaugh**

•"I've had some Democrat African-American leaders tell me they're really not all that comfortable with Obama as the lead at the MLK festivities 'cause he's not down for the struggle. He does not have that in his roots."
-- **Rush Limbaugh**

•"I will be the first to admit that getting votes and getting an audience are two different things. For example, a politician really can't be elected if he's hated by half the people. A talk show host, however, can be an overwhelming national phenomenon while being hated by half the people."
-- **Rush Limbaugh**

•"I want anyone who believes in life, liberty, pursuit of happiness to succeed. And I want any force, any person, any element of an overarching Big Government that would stop your success, I want that organization, that element or that person to fail. I want you to succeed."
-- **Rush Limbaugh**

• "I never open the newspaper, never. I never go to a website; I never turn on the T.V. hoping to find something I can attack. It isn't what I do. I defend."
-- **Rush Limbaugh**

- "I had to learn early on that where conservatives are concerned, the truth about them is the last thing anybody wants to report. It's the lies and distortions, the mischaracterizations, the character assassinations, that people want to report."
-- **Rush Limbaugh**

•"I do not believe that Obama is smarter than anybody else. I do not believe he has cut a new path and is a politician unlike any we've ever seen regarding his intellect. I don't believe any of this hocus-pocus. I didn't believe it when they said it about Hillary, Smartest Woman in the World."
-- **Rush Limbaugh**

•"I can't tell you the number of times in high school I was allowed to be disappointed for not making the grade; it's a part of life. So the young students who are being taught by radical leftists in this country today are going to end up growing up in a world for which they are totally unprepared and unequipped."
-- **Rush Limbaugh**

•"The idea of going back to college scares me, and I didn't even go. I went to college for one year, two semesters. If you add up the total time, I probably didn't even go one semester."
-- **Rush Limbaugh**

Made in the USA
Monee, IL
21 November 2022

18038599R00066